# READY, STEADY, PRACTISE!

Laura Griffiths

## Grammar & Punctuation
Pupil Book **Year 5**

# Features of this book

- Clear explanations and worked examples for each grammar & punctuation topic from the KS2 National Curriculum.

- Questions split into three sections that become progressively more challenging:

Warm up

Test yourself

Challenge yourself

- 'How did you do?' checks at the end of each topic for self-evaluation.

- Regular progress tests to assess pupils' understanding and recap on their learning.

- Answers to every question in a pull-out section at the centre of the book.

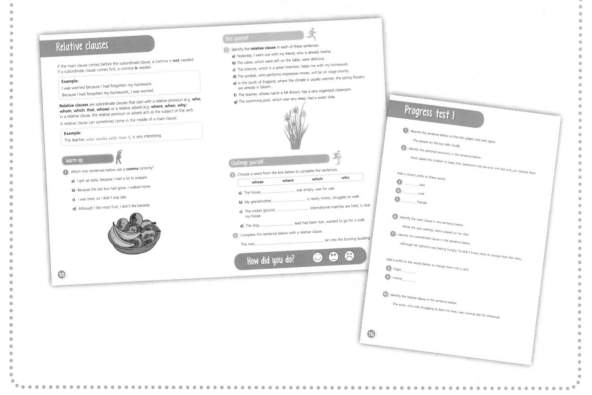

# Contents

Prefixes 4

Suffixes 6

Clauses 8

Relative clauses 10

Relative pronouns 12

Subject and verb agreement 14

*Progress test 1* 16

Adverbs to show possibility 18

Adverbials of time 20

Adverbials of place 22

Conjunctions 24

Modal verbs 26

Connectives 28

*Progress test 2* 30

Brackets and dashes 32

Commas 1 34

Commas 2 36

Paragraphs 38

Direct speech 40

*Progress test 3* 42

*Answers (centre pull-out)* 1–4

# Prefixes

A **prefix** is added at the **beginning** of a word. This turns it into a new word.

A verb prefix is a prefix that is added to a verb.

**Examples:**

**re**play     **un**helpful     **over**take     **mis**behave     **de**compose

The most common prefixes are **un**, **de**, **dis**, **re**, **pre** and **mis**. These prefixes have meanings.

**un** = not          **de** = making the opposite          **dis** = the opposite
**re** = again          **pre** = before          **mis** = wrong

## Warm up

1) Write out these words and then decide whether to add **un** or **dis** to them to change their meaning.

   **a)** certain                    **b)** agree

   **c)** qualify                     **d)** appear

   **e)** do                            **f)** seen

   **g)** infect                       **h)** obey

2) Write a sentence using each word below to show you understand the meaning with and without the prefix.

   **a)** tie

   **b)** untie

   **c)** dress

   **d)** undress

   **e)** aware

   **f)** unaware

**3** Write out these verbs using a correct prefix.
Choose either **un**, **dis**, **de**, **re**, **mis** or **pre**.

**a)** understand **b)** fill

**c)** embark **d)** pick

**e)** do **f)** like

**g)** tidy **h)** call

**4** Copy the sentences, completing each with a correct prefix.

**a)** I _____ like the cold weather in winter.

**b)** Sometimes my mum _____ heats the soup and it burns!

**c)** I keep making _____ takes on my homework.

**d)** The twin girls are feeling _____ happy.

**e)** Can I buy a _____ turn ticket?

## Challenge yourself

**5** Copy and complete the table, writing as many words as you can with the prefixes shown in the first column. An example has been done for you.

| un | unhappy |
|---|---|
| dis | |
| pre | |
| over | |

## How did you do?

# Suffixes

A **noun** is an object. An **adjective** is a word that describes an object.

**Examples:**

The green grass moved in the breeze.

**(adjective)  (noun)**

Sometimes a noun can be changed into a verb using a **suffix**.

A suffix is group of letters added to the end of a word to change its meaning.

Common suffixes which do this are **ate** and **ise**.

**Examples:**

The chef's **speciality** is curry.        The chef **specialises** in curry.

The suffix **en** and **ify** are used to change some adjectives into verbs.

**Examples:**

tight (adjective) – tight**en** (verb)        intense (adjective – intens**ify** (verb)

When the suffix ends in an **e** remember to take the take the **e** off before adding the suffix.

Warm up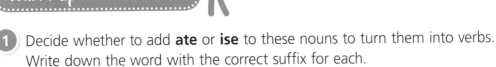

1. Decide whether to add **ate** or **ise** to these nouns to turn them into verbs. Write down the word with the correct suffix for each.

   **a)** captive                 **b)** terror

   **c)** motive                  **d)** author

   **e)** saliva                  **f)** economy

2. Decide whether to add **en** or **ify** to these adjectives to turn them into verbs. Write down the word with the correct suffix for each.

   **a)** fright                  **b)** simple

   **c)** note                    **d)** sad

   **e)** length                  **f)** intense

**3** Copy and complete these sentences, choosing the correct word from the list below.

| | | | |
|---|---|---|---|
| **apologise** | **magnify** | **qualify** | **frighten** |
| **brighten** | **specialise** | **verify** | |

**a)** We hope to _____ for the World Cup.

**b)** We will need to _____ the signature.

**c)** The day will _____ up after lunch.

**d)** I can _____ in maths when I am older.

**e)** My new glasses will _____ the words in my book.

**f)** The giant will _____ Jack away.

**g)** _____ to your brother for breaking his toy.

**Challenge yourself**

**4** Look at these nouns and adjectives.
Add a suffix to change each word into a verb, and then write a sentence that shows you know the meaning of the verb.

**a)** summary

**b)** light

**c)** fortune

**d)** humid

## How did you do?

# Clauses

A **clause** is a group of words that contains at least one **subject** and one **verb**.

**Example:**

main clause

**Uzma plays** football.

subject    verb

A **main clause** is a complete sentence that makes sense by itself.

**Subordinate clauses** still have a subject and a verb but they start with a **subordinating conjunction** and so do not make sense on their own. They need to be paired with a main clause.

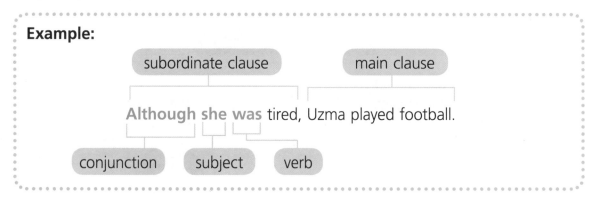

**Example:**

subordinate clause          main clause

**Although she was** tired, Uzma played football.

conjunction    subject    verb

## Warm up

1  Copy each sentence, and underline the **main clause**.

a) The baby drank some milk.

b) The boy sat down until the bus arrived.

c) Because he was tired, Jonah went to bed.

d) I must wear my hat, as it is a hot day.

**2** Draw the table below. Decide if each clause is a main or subordinate clause and write it in the correct place in the table.

**before we left**     **I baked a cake**     **because we are on holiday**

**we will have a BBQ**     **our dog can perform tricks**     **despite the heat**

| Main clauses | Subordinate clauses |
|---|---|
|  |  |
|  |  |
|  |  |
|  |  |
|  |  |

**Challenge yourself**

**3** Copy and complete these sentences by adding a **main clause**.

**a)** After a long day at work, _____

**b)** Although it was his birthday, _____

**c)** _____ because he was slow.

**d)** _____ while she ate her tea.

**4** Copy and complete the sentence below by adding a **subordinate clause**.

The girl cried _____ .

# Relative clauses

If the main clause comes before the subordinate clause, a comma is **not** needed.
If a subordinate clause comes first, a comma **is** needed.

> **Example:**
>
> I was worried because I had forgotten my homework.
>
> Because I had forgotten my homework**,** I was worried.

**Relative clauses** are subordinate clauses that start with a relative pronoun (e.g. **who**, **whom**, **which**, **that**, **whose**) or a relative adverb (e.g. **where**, **when**, **why**).
In a relative clause, the relative pronoun or adverb acts as the subject of the verb.

A relative clause can sometimes come in the middle of a main clause.

> **Example:**
>
> The teacher, who works with Year 5, is very interesting.

## Warm up

1. Which two sentences below use a **comma** correctly?

   **a)** I got up early, because I had a lot to prepare.

   **b)** Because the last bus had gone, I walked home.

   **c)** I was tired, so I didn't stay late.

   **d)** Although I like most fruit, I don't like bananas.

**2** Identify the **relative clause** in each of these sentences.

**a)** Yesterday, I went out with my friend, who is already twelve.

**b)** The cakes, which were left on the table, were delicious.

**c)** The Internet, which is a great invention, helps me with my homework.

**d)** The acrobat, who performs impressive moves, will be on stage shortly.

**e)** In the south of England, where the climate is usually warmer, the spring flowers are already in bloom.

**f)** The teacher, whose name is Mr Brown, has a very organised classroom.

**g)** The swimming pool, which was very deep, had a water slide.

Challenge yourself

**3** Choose a word from the box below to complete the sentences.

| whose | where | which | who |
|---|---|---|---|

**a)** The house, _____ was empty, was for sale.

**b)** My grandmother, _____ is nearly ninety, struggles to walk.

**c)** The cricket ground, _____ international matches are held, is near my house.

**d)** The dog, _____ lead had been lost, wanted to go for a walk.

**4** Complete the sentence below with a relative clause.

The man, _____, ran into the burning building.

## How did you do?

# Relative pronouns

**Personal pronouns**, which take the place of a noun, can vary depending on whether they are the subject or object of a sentence.

| Subject | I | you | she | he | it | we | they |
|---|---|---|---|---|---|---|---|
| Object | me | you | her | him | it | us | them |

Listed below are some **relative pronouns**.

**that**       **which**       **who**       **whom**

**whose**       **whichever**       **whoever**       **whomever**

Relative pronouns link a **subordinate** clause to the rest of the sentence.
A subordinate clause has a subject and a verb but starts with a subordinating conjunction, e.g. **although**, **despite**, **when**, **whose**.

> **Example:**
>
> The children, whose parents were on holiday, were staying with their friends.

**Warm up**

1) Look at the sentences below and write down whether each one uses a personal or relative pronoun.

   **a)** Alex loved his football.

   **b)** Sarah and I had lunch together.

   **c)** The banana, which was ripe, was ready to eat.

   **d)** The fish that were swimming in the pond needed feeding.

   **e)** "Can you throw his ball back, please?"

   **f)** The dancers, who were about to go on stage, suddenly felt nervous.

   **g)** The teachers, whose job it was to care for their students, worked hard.

2 Choose a suitable relative pronoun for each sentence.

**a)** The books, _____ are kept in school, are new.

**b)** Madrid, _____ is the capital of Spain, is the home of two main football teams.

**c)** William Shakespeare, _____ wrote famous plays, lived in Stratford-upon-Avon.

**d)** The doctor, _____ surgery is nearby, will be arriving at 6 p.m.

**e)** The leisure centre asks that _____ watches swimming lessons, removes their shoes.

**f)** The train fare is increasing for those _____ travel after 3 p.m.

**Challenge yourself**

3 Identify the correct relative pronoun in each of these sentences.

**a)** The lifeguard, **whose / which** job it is to watch the pool, needs to be fit.

**b)** Police, **that / who** work in the community are there to help us.

**c)** The pirates **who / which** lived on a faraway island, were looking for treasure.

**d)** "The photographer needs **whose / whoever** belongs to the Wright family to stand by the gate, please!"

**e)** The man, **whose / whom** name is Freddie, likes listening to the radio.

**f)** The head teacher told all the children **that / whose** were in Year 5 not to bring sweets to school.

4 Write a sentence of your own using a relative pronoun.

**How did you do?**

# Subject and verb agreement

Most sentences have a **subject** and a **verb**. The subject is normally the person or thing that is doing the action. The verb is the doing (or sometimes being) word.

**Example:**

You play cricket with a bat and ball.

subject    verb

You need to be sure that the subject **agrees** with the verb.

**Examples:**

| ✓ | ✗ |
|---|---|
| I like cricket. | I likes cricket. |
| You are learning to play. | You is learning to play. |
| The girl looks for the ball. | The girl look for the ball. |
| We play cricket. | We plays cricket. |

## Warm up

1  Which sentences are grammatically correct?

a) We is going to the shops.

b) The children have gone to the lake.

c) I done my homework.

d) You drive really well.

e) They spends the most money.

f) The man know a lot about computers.

**2** Choose the correct form of the verb in each sentence below.

**a)** Sarah and Tamara **have** / **has** brown hair.

**b)** My brother **ride** / **rides** his bike all the time.

**c)** You **play** / **plays** on your computer every night.

**d)** I **is** / **am** going to put the rubbish in the bin.

**Challenge yourself**

**3** Rewrite these sentences, changing either the form of the subject **or** the form of the verb, so that they agree.

**Example:** The monkey swing through the trees.

*Two possible answers*: The monkey swing**s** through the trees **or**
The monkey**s** swing through the trees.

**a)** The sheep dog are chasing the flock of sheep.

**b)** The shops is closing for lunch and will reopen at 2 p.m.

**c)** The babies keeps crying because they wants some more milk.

**d)** The children has finished the game.

**e)** The bag of sandwiches were left behind this morning.

**How did you do?**

**1** Rewrite the sentence below so that the subject and verb agree.

The people on the bus talks loudly.

**2** Identify the personal pronouns in the sentence below.

Mum asked the children to keep their bedrooms tidy because she had only just cleaned them.

Add a correct prefix to these words.

**3** _____take

**4** _____cook

**5** _____friendly

**6** Identify the main clause in the sentence below.

While she was waiting, Leena played on her iPad.

**7** Identify the subordinate clause in the sentence below.

Although Mr Salmons was feeling hungry, he didn't know what to choose from the menu.

Add a suffix to the words below to change them into a verb.

**8** fright_____

**9** motive_____

**10** Identify the relative clause in the sentence below.

The actor, who was struggling to learn his lines, was running late for rehearsals.

**11** Write down the relative pronoun that was used in question 10.

**12** What is the subordinate clause in this sentence?

Despite being only eleven, Faith was solving maths problems that were very difficult.

Write three words that start with the prefix **mis**.

**13** mis_____

**14** mis_____

**15** mis_____

**16** What does the prefix **mis** mean?

**17** Choose the correct relative pronoun for the sentence below.

The computer, _____was very old and needed replacing, wouldn't work this morning.

**18** Write out two subordinate clauses to the main clause below.

_____ I wore my hat and gloves _____

Write two sentences each containing a relative clause.

**19** _____

**20** _____

Score ⬤/ 20

# Adverbs to show possibility

**Adverbs** can be used to show the **possibility** of something happening.

**Example:**

perhaps, surely, certainly, probably, maybe, clearly, definitely, possibly

The adverbs **perhaps** and **maybe** are usually written at the beginning of the clause.

**Example:**

Perhaps the washing will dry outside.

Adverbs usually come before the main verb.

**Example:**

The washing will probably dry outside.

 **Warm up**

1 Look at each group of adverbs which show possibility.

Write them out, putting them in order starting with the **most certain** likelihood of something happening.

a) possibly, definitely, unlikely

b) certainly, possibly, probably

c) maybe, possibly, definitely

**2** Write down the adverb of probability in each sentence.

**a)** I will definitely go to the music festival next year.

**b)** It is unlikely I will be going on holiday in the New Year.

**c)** Maybe the rain will stop this afternoon.

**d)** Perhaps it will be my turn next.

**e)** The dog is probably going to chase after the stick.

**f)** Undoubtedly, he is a great athlete.

**3** Rewrite the sentences in each set in the order in which they are likely to happen. Start with the least likely.

**a)** I will watch TV tonight.

Maybe I will watch TV tonight.

I will possibly watch TV tonight.

I will definitely watch TV tonight.

**b)** Perhaps you should wash it first.

You should certainly wash it first.

You should probably wash it first.

You should clearly wash it first.

## Challenge yourself

**4** Complete these sentences using an adverb of possibility.

**a)** It is _____ going to rain.

**b)** My friends will _____ come to play at my house.

**c)** _____ I will be chosen to sing a solo.

**d)** I will _____ be watching the football match on Sunday.

**e)** It will _____ take a long time, will _____ be difficult but _____ I will try it!

**5** Write your own sentence using an adverb to show possibility.

## How did you do?

# Adverbials of time

An **adverbial of time** is a type of adverb or adverbial phrase. It is used to give more information about the **time** or **frequency** of an action.

Adverbials of time are useful to use in your writing because they give added detail, provide chronological sequencing and can move stories forwards or create flashbacks.

> **Example:**
>
> **Eventually**, he arrived at the house. He **rarely** visited it as it made him sad, but **lately** he had started to feel that **sooner or later** he must do so.

**Adverbials of probability** show how certain we are about something. Common ones are: **certainly**, **definitely**, **maybe**, **perhaps** and **possibly**.

> **Example:**
>
> It will **certainly** take a long time, will **probably** be difficult, but **maybe** I will try it.

## Warm up

**1** Write down all the **adverbials of time**, from the list below.

| after a while | beautifully | previously |
| soon | tightly | quietly | before |
| instantly | openly | immediately | secretly |

**2** Complete these sentences with an adverbial of time.

   **a)** We expect our cousins to arrive _____.

   **b)** _____, the sun was shining.

   **c)** My mum can pick us up _____.

3 Copy the table below. Then sort the adverbials below into adverbials of time and adverbials of probability.

**certainly**    **soon**     **afterwards**     **possibly**     **seldom**

**next week**     **maybe**     **perhaps**     **last night**     **all day**

| Adverbials of time | Adverbials of probability |
|---|---|
| | |
| | |
| | |
| | |

**Challenge yourself**

4 Write the first paragraph of a story using at least four adverbials of time. Underline each one.

5 Write the first part of an autobiography. Remember to write in chronological order and use adverbials of time. Underline each example you use.

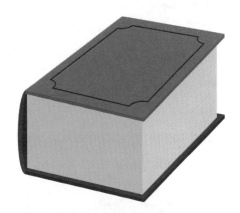

**How did you do?**

# Adverbials of place

**Adverbials of place** describe the location.

**Examples:**

nearby, outside, inside, downstairs, abroad, anywhere, somewhere, there

**Prepositions** are used to describe where someone or something is.

**Examples:**

The cat is **in the basket**.

The chair is **next to the door**.

Adverbials can also be used to show distance.

**Examples:**

Majorca is 260 miles **away from** mainland Spain.

The car is parked 100 m **from** the entrance.

**Warm up**

1) Identify the adverbial of place used in each sentence.

   **a)** Shall we wait inside the restaurant for a table?

   **b)** I left my school bag downstairs.

   **c)** I'm happy to go anywhere on holiday.

   **d)** Is there a car park nearby?

   **e)** Look over there and read the sign on the door.

   **f)** I am going out with my friends tonight.

   **g)** Can you cross over the road, please?

   **h)** We need to be able to cartwheel backwards to get our gym badge.

# Answers

## Pages 4–5

1. a) uncertain    b) disagree
   c) disqualify    d) disappear
   e) undo    f) unseen
   g) disinfect    h) disobey
2. **Any correct sentence, which uses the word correctly. For example:**
   a) I can tie my shoelaces.
   b) My sister likes to untie her shoelaces all the time!
   c) We have to dress in smart clothes for a party.
   d) Before bed, I have to undress myself and put my pyjamas on.
   e) I am aware of the issues in the news today.
   f) My brother, however, is unaware and shows no interest in current issues in the news.
3. a) misunderstand    b) refill
   c) disembark    d) unpick
   e) undo / redo    f) unlike / dislike
   g) untidy    h) recall
4. a) dislike    b) over
   c) mistakes    d) unhappy
   e) return
5. **Accept any correct words. For example:**
   undone, unloved, unfixed, unkind.
   disobey, disagree, dislike, disinterest, disprove.
   prehistoric, prewash, preheat, preview.
   overdone, overexcite, overturn, overcook, overrun.

## Pages 6–7

1. a) captivate    b) terrorise
   c) motivate    d) authorise
   e) salivate    f) economise
2. a) frighten    b) simplify
   c) notify    d) sadden
   e) lengthen    f) intensify
3. a) qualify    b) verify
   c) brighten    d) specialise
   e) magnify    f) frighten
   g) Apologise
4. **Any sentence using the verb. For example:**
   a) Summarise – I will summarise the main points for you.
   b) Lighten – The pale walls lighten the room / Taking out the books will lighten your bag.
   c) Fortunate – I was fortunate to win the lottery.
   d) Humidify – We can humidify the room.

## Pages 8–9

1. a) The baby drank some milk.
   b) The boy sat down until the bus arrived.
   c) Because he was tired, Jonah went to bed.
   d) I must wear my hat, as it is a hot day.
2. 

| Main clauses | Subordinate clauses |
|---|---|
| • we will have a BBQ | • before we left |
| • our dog can perform tricks | • despite the heat |
| • I baked a cake | • because we are on holiday |

3. a)–d) **Accept any grammatically correct main clauses. For example:** After a long day at work, **he read a book**.
4. **Accept any grammatically correct subordinate clause. For example:** The girl cried **because she hurt her knee**.

## Pages 10–11

1. b) Because the last bus had gone, I walked home;
   d) Although I like most fruit, I don't like bananas.
2. a) Yesterday, I went out with my friend, who is already twelve.
   b) The cakes, which were left on the table, were delicious.
   c) The Internet, which is a great invention, helps me with my homework.
   d) The acrobat, who performs impressive moves, will be on stage shortly.
   e) In the south of England, where the climate is usually warmer, the spring flowers are already in bloom.
   f) The teacher, whose name is Mr Brown, has a very organised classroom.
   g) The swimming pool, which is very deep, had a water slide.
3. a) which    b) who
   c) where    d) whose
4. **Accept any grammatically correct relative clause. For example:** The man, who had just heard his daughter, ran into the burning building.

## Pages 12–13

1. a) personal    b) personal
   c) relative    d) relative
   e) personal    f) relative
   g) relative
2. **Any suitable pronoun. For example:**
   a) which
   b) which
   c) who
   d) whose
   e) whoever
   f) who
3. a) whose    b) who
   c) who    d) whoever
   e) whose    f) that
4. **Any suitable sentence that includes a relative pronoun.** For example: Pupils **who** wish to run the race must bring their PE kit.

## Pages 14–15

1. The children have gone to the lake;
   You drive really well.
2. a) have    b) rides
   c) play    d) am
3. a) The **sheep dog is / sheep dogs are** chasing the flock of sheep.
   b) The **shops are / shop is** closing for lunch and will reopen at 2 p.m.
   c) The **babies keep crying / baby keeps crying** because **they want / it wants** some more milk.
   d) The **children have / child has** finished the game.
   e) The **bag of sandwiches was / bags of sandwiches were** left behind this morning.

## Pages 16–17

1. The people on the bus talk loudly.
2. Mum asked the children to keep their bedrooms tidy because she had only just cleaned them.
3. mistake
4. overcook
5. unfriendly
6. While she was waiting, Leena played on her iPad.
7. Although Mr Salmons was feeling hungry, he didn't know what to choose from the menu.
8. frighten
9. motivate

10. The actor, <u>who was struggling to learn his lines</u>, was running late for rehearsals.
11. who
12. Despite being only eleven
13–15. **Any correct words starting with mis. For example:** mistake, misunderstand, mislead, mistreat, misfortune, misprint
16. wrong
17. which
18. **Any suitable subordinate clauses. For example:** <u>Because it was cold</u>, I wore my hat and gloves <u>while I was playing outside.</u>
19–20. **Any suitable sentences that use a relative clause. For example:** The children, <u>who had finished their tests</u>, went to play outside.

**Pages 18–19**
1. a) definitely, possibly, unlikely
   b) certainly, probably, possibly
   c) definitely, possibly, maybe
2. a) definitely
   b) unlikely
   c) maybe
   d) perhaps
   e) probably
   f) undoubtedly
3. a) I will possibly watch TV tonight.
      Maybe I will watch TV tonight.
      I will watch TV tonight.
      I will definitely watch TV tonight.
   b) Perhaps you should wash it first.
      You should probably wash it first.
      You should certainly wash it first.
      You should clearly wash it first.
4. **Any suitable adverb of possibility. For example:**
   a) possibly
   b) perhaps
   c) maybe / perhaps
   d) probably
   e) probably, surely, maybe
5. **Any sentence to include an adverb of probability. For example:** I will certainly do well in a grammar test!

**Pages 20–21**
1. after a while, previously, soon, before, instantly, immediately
2. a)–c) **Accept any suitable adverbials of time. For example:** soon, previously, next week
3.

| Adverbials of time | Adverbials of probability |
|---|---|
| soon, afterwards, seldom, next week, last night, all day | certainly, possibly, maybe, perhaps |

4. **Any paragraph using four or more adverbials of time. For example:** yesterday, last year, in the future, next term
5. Any writing in the style of an autobiography, with correct use of adverbials of time underlined. e.g. after, later, before etc.

**Pages 22–23**
1. a) inside
   b) downstairs
   c) anywhere
   d) nearby
   e) there
   f) out
   g) over
   h) backwards

2. a) behind
   b) abroad
   c) indoors
   d) above
   e) south
   f) away
   g) towards
   h) upstairs
3. **Any suitable answer – e.g.**
   a) The fair is nearby.
   b) Let's play there on the beach.
   c) The aeroplane is flying high above the ground.
   d) Can you skip backwards?
   e) Which way is north?
   f) I am looking for somewhere to play.

**Pages 24–25**
1. a) and          b) or
   c) so           d) for
2. a) because      b) Although
   c) When         d) Since
   e) before
3. **Accept any grammatically correct clauses linked by one of the connectives. For example:**
   a) He rode his bike **but I walked**.
   b) **Nobody was in when I** went home.
   c) Our teacher was ill **until Monday**.
   d) **If you are good**, you can have an ice cream.
   e) At the show I won **and I cried**.
   f) There are not many people **so it will be quiet**.

**Pages 26–27**
1. a) Shall        b) could
   c) should       d) would
   e) might
2. a) should       b) will
   c) ought        d) will
   e) ought
3. a)–c) **Accept any suitable and grammatically correct endings.**
4. a)–d) **Accept any suitable and grammatically correct beginnings containing a modal verb and a noun.**

**Pages 28–29**
1. a) Tigers are beautiful. However, don't try to pat one.
2. a) Also         b) however
   c) Consequently d) Firstly
3. a) to contrast  b) to sequence
   c) to summarise d) to contrast
   e) to sequence  f) to summarise
4. a) It's too late to go shopping. **Besides**, I'm tired.
   b) Many towns are on a river. **For instance**, London is on the Thames.
   c) We could go for a picnic tomorrow. **Ultimately**, the weather will decide.

**Pages 30–31**
1–2. Any suitable adverb. For example: onto, over
3. **Any suitable adverbial of time. For example:** after a while
4. b) An adverbial of possibility.
5. <u>Finally</u> the children were asleep.
6. <u>Meanwhile</u>, all we could do was wait.
7. **Any suitable adverbial of possibility For example:** probably / perhaps / maybe
8. Finally
9. might, must, will
10–12. **Any suitable modal verbs. For example:** should, must, could/would/should
13. In the final paragraph.

**14.** We are running <u>towards the sea</u>.

**15.** John moved <u>away from the snake</u> very slowly.

**16.-17.** **Any suitable sentences. For example:**
The children should eat all their dinner.
We shall be running in a race tomorrow.

**18.** All the class could pass if they work well.

**19.** because

**20.** **Any from the following:** by using paragraphs / subheadings / headings / use of adverbials of time

## Pages 32–33

**1.** The music concert (in the local theatre) starts at five o'clock.
The programme (about whales) was very interesting.

**2.** a) Washington (in America) is where the President lives.
   b) Ice skating (although it is a bit dangerous) is lots of fun.
   c) Galleons (Tudor ships) were very big and slow.
   d) Erin is a great singer (or so she thinks!).
   e) February (often rainy) is the coldest month of the year.

**3.** a)–c) **Accept any three of the following:**
Washington – in America – is where the President lives.
Ice skating – although it is a bit dangerous – is lots of fun.
Galleons – Tudor ships – were very big and slow.
Erin is a great singer – or so she thinks!
February – often rainy – is the coldest month of the year.

**4.** a) My birthday, on August 29th, makes me the youngest girl in my class.
   b) The sun, normally hiding, was shining yesterday.

## Pages 34–35

**1.** a) I like English, geography, science, music and art.
   b) Newcastle, Liverpool, Hartlepool and Leeds are all in the north of England.
   c) The Nile, Amazon, Mississippi, Congo and Amur are some of the world's longest rivers.
   d) For lunch we ate sandwiches, crisps, some cucumber and tomato, and a biscuit.
   e) My friends are called Amos, Seb, Summer and Raj.
   f) The cinema is only open on a Friday, Saturday, Sunday and Wednesday.

**2.** a) The children, who were all aged 10, played at the park.
   b) The boy stopped talking, had a drink, then started again!
   c) When we arrived at the airport, we found our flight had been cancelled.
   d) I like skipping, but my brother likes football.
   e) My friends are all going ice skating, but I have to go to the dentist.
   f) Although I am good at spelling, I still need to use a dictionary sometimes.
   g) Our school, which is one hundred years old, had a special party.

**3.** **Any suitable sentences. For example:**
   a) Our garden, which is fairly small, faces south.
   b) The bus station, in the centre of town, was very busy.
   c) My cousins, Emily and Zane, are coming to stay for a few days.
   d) The doctor, who is based at the health centre, arrived at the hospital.
   e) My birthday present, which is wrapped beautifully, is in my bedroom.
   f) My mum, who likes keeping fit, was going to the gym.

## Pages 36–37

**1.** a) **i)** Two **ii)** Three   b) **i)** Three **ii)** Two
   c) **i)** Five **ii)** Three

**2.** **Ensure pictures show all items clearly.**
   a) chocolate cake, fruit cake, strawberries.
   b) chocolate, cake, fruit cake, strawberries

---

   c) picture of someone trying to eat Grandma
   d) picture of people having dinner with Grandma.

**3.** a) Help police   b) Help, police!

**4.** **Two sentences that shows knowledge of how changing the position of commas in a sentence can change its meaning.**

## Pages 38–39

**1.** a) non-fiction      b) fiction
   c) fiction           d) non-fiction
   e) non-fiction        f) fiction
   g) non-fiction        h) non-fiction.

**2.** **Any suitable sentences keeping the theme of the paragraph.**

**3.** **Any fact sheet where ideas are grouped into paragraphs.**

## Pages 40–41

**1.** "Where's your homework?" the teacher asked.
"If you finish," he said, "you'll make me very proud."

**2.** a) Abbey said, "Don't worry."
   b) "Nothing is wrong," replied Dad.
   c) "Maybe one day," said Josh, "we'll play football for England!"
   d) "Help!" shouted the lost little girl. "Help!"

**3.** a) Holly said, "I can't wait to go on holiday next year." /
      "I can't wait to go on holiday next year," Holly said.
   b) Alfie told his teacher, "I don't understand the work." /
      "I don't understand the work," Alfie told his teacher.
   c) The reporter announced, "The restaurant has been shut down because of hygiene issues." / "The restaurant has been shut down because of hygiene issues," the reporter announced.

## Pages 42–43

**1.** Football, golf, tennis and cricket are my favourite sports.

**2.** A balanced diet, which includes fruit and vegetables, helps us to keep healthy.

**3.** a) The politician announced, "We will open new schools."

**4.** Sarah (aged 11) produced some excellent artwork in the style of Monet (a famous artist).

**5.** Mario (from Wolverhampton) was last seen walking his dog in the park (near the community centre).

**6.** "There was a burglary this afternoon between the hours of 14.00 and 18.00. I am looking for witnesses," said the detective

**7.** "You need to arrest this man immediately," the detective advised the chief inspector.

**8–9.** **Any correct sentences using brackets.**
   **For example:** A dog has fallen into a pond (at the park).

**10.** November, December, January and February are all winter months.

**11.** Cats, rabbits, dogs, fish, gerbils and hamsters are all pets.

**12.** I have visited lots of places including France, Germany, Spain and Italy.

**13.** Stop! Ducks crossing road.

**14.** Computer games online can become quite addictive – parents are warned.

**15.** The temperature – according to the Met office – is going to be higher than yesterday.

**16.** All children must write a letter – as mentioned in assembly last week – to invite their parents into school. **or** All children must write a letter, as mentioned in assembly last week, to invite their parents into school.

**17.** The school trip (taking place in July) will be a four-night residential.

**18.** My car (a silver Vauxhall) is at the garage.

**19.** Reporters (local and national) are at the scene.

**20.** organise

**2** Complete each sentence using one of the adverbials below. Use each word only once.

away    towards    abroad    indoors

upstairs    behind    above    south

**a)** Stand _____ the line, please and wait for me to call your name.

**b)** We are going _____ on holiday next year.

**c)** The plants _____ will need watering every week.

**d)** The seats in the theatre _____ the stage were the most expensive.

**e)** Some birds fly _____ in the winter.

**f)** "Go _____ !" I shouted at my brother.

**g)** We ran _____ the exit.

**h)** My bedroom is _____ at the top of the house.

**Challenge yourself**

**3** Write a sentence for each of the adverbials of place below.
   **a)** nearby
   **b)** there
   **c)** above
   **d)** backwards
   **e)** north
   **f)** somewhere

**How did you do?**

# Conjunctions

**Conjunctions** are a type of **connective**. They are used to connect words, phrases and clauses together.

> **Examples:**
>
> I like apples **and** oranges.       I like apples **but** not oranges.

Conjunctions come in two types. The **coordinating conjunctions** are **and**, **but**, **for**, **so**, **yet**, **or**, **nor**. They can be used to link **two main clauses** of equal importance.

> **Example:**
>
> I like apples **and** I like oranges.

**Subordinating conjunctions** (**although**, **because**, **if**, **since**, **when** and many more) connect a **main clause** to a **subordinate clause**. Remember that a subordinate clause does not make sense on its own.

> **Example:**
>
> I like apples **because** they are good for me.

Subordinating conjunctions can often come at the start of a sentence.

> **Example:**
>
> **Although** I don't eat much fruit, I like apples.

## Warm up

**1** What is the **coordinating conjunction** in each sentence below?

**a)** He plays rugby and tennis.

**b)** Joshua or Simon can help you.

**c)** Take the umbrella so we won't get wet.

**d)** You should listen for you might learn something.

**2** What is the **subordinating conjunction** in each sentence?

**a)** Go to the exhibition because it is really interesting.

**b)** Although it is sunny, it might rain later.

**c)** When it is my birthday, I will be eleven.

**d)** Since you are still finishing your homework, I will play on my own.

**e)** I want to learn how to ice skate before I go on holiday.

## Challenge yourself

**3** Using one of the conjunctions in the box, copy and complete the sentences below with a **main** or **subordinate clause**. Use each connective once and remember that a clause must contain a **verb** and a **noun**.

| and | but | if | so | until | when |
|-----|-----|-----|-----|-------|------|

**a)** He rode his bike _____.

**b)** _____ I went home.

**c)** Our teacher was ill _____.

**d)** _____ you can have an ice cream.

**e)** At the show I won _____.

**f)** There are not many people _____.

## How did you do?

# Modal verbs

The main modal verbs are **will**, **would**, **can**, **could**, **may**, **might**, **shall**, **should**, **must** and **ought**.

Modal verbs can express necessity, uncertainty, ability or permission.

**Example:**

less certain     I **might** do my homework.

&darr;          I **should** do my homework.

more certain    I **will** do my homework.

To talk about the past using a modal verb we add **have + the past participle of the verb** (often the form of the verb ending in **ed**).

**Example:**

I **might have played** outside.

modal verb        past participle

I **should have done** my homework.

modal verb        past participle

## Warm up

**1** Find the modal verb in each sentence below.

**a)** Shall we go out for dinner tonight?

**b)** We could have caught the bus.

**c)** They should work harder in training.

**d)** The kittens would have been hungry if you hadn't fed them.

**e)** You might see me because I will be wearing a red top hat.

2 Choose the correct modal verbs below so that the sentences make sense.

a) He really **should / ought** save some money.

b) If you want to go ice skating you **ought / will** need to hire some skates.

c) I **ought / shall** to go to bed earlier because I am always tired.

d) I **will / ought** do my homework.

e) I **shall / ought** to eat more fruit and fewer sweets!

3 Complete these sentences so that they say something about your school.

**Example:** You must pay attention in class.

a) You ought to … .

b) You can … .

c) You should … .

4 Copy and complete these sentences using a **different noun** and a **different modal verb** at the beginning of each.

**Example:** Tomorrow will be cold.

a) _____ be good.

b) _____ be exciting.

c) _____ be boring.

d) _____ be dangerous.

# How did you do?

# Connectives

A **connective** is a linking word or phrase. Connectives can link words, clauses and phrases together in a single sentence. They can also link together **different** sentences. In this way they add cohesion to a text.

**Example:**

The train broke down. Therefore, we were late.

The connective does not have to come at the beginning of the second sentence. It can act as a link to the first sentence from other positions.

**Example:**

The train broke down. We were therefore late.

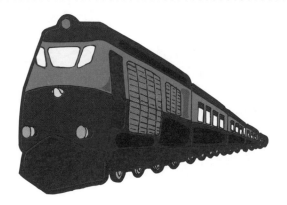

Connectives make writing more interesting and can be grouped into types according to their function. Here are some important types with examples:

| Function of connective | Examples |
|---|---|
| to contrast | however; although |
| to add | also; furthermore |
| to sequence | firstly; finally |
| to give examples | for instance; such as |
| to show results | therefore; consequently |
| to summarise | overall; to conclude |

**1** Which example below is linked by a connective?

    **a)** Tigers are beautiful. However, don't try to pat one.

    **b)** Tigers are amazing. We should protect them.

    **c)** Tigers eat meat. Tigers can be dangerous.

## Test yourself

**2** What is the connective in each of the sentences below?

    **a)** The fair was exciting. Also, it was cheap.

    **b)** My brother played chess; however, I watched a film.

    **c)** I went to the library. Consequently, I have lots of books to read.

    **d)** It wasn't a good idea to go. Firstly, it was too far away.

## Challenge yourself

**3** Say whether each connective below would be used **to contrast**, **to sequence** or **to summarise**.

    **a)** whereas           **b)** secondly

    **c)** all in all        **d)** however

    **e)** to begin with   **f)** overall

**4** Copy the sentences below. Use the connectives in the box to fill in the gaps.

| For instance | Besides | Ultimately |
| --- | --- | --- |

    **a)** It's too late to go shopping. _____, I'm tired.

    **b)** Many towns are on a river. _____, London is on the Thames.

    **c)** We could go for a picnic tomorrow. _____, the weather will decide.

# How did you do?

29

# Progress test 2

Think of an adverbial of place to complete each sentence below.

**1** The sea crashed _____ the rocks.

**2** The naughty puppy jumped _____ the table and broke the vase.

**3** Write down an adverbial of time.

**4** What type of adverbial is **perhaps**? Choose one from the list below.

**a)** An adverbial of place.

**b)** An adverbial of possibility.

**c)** An adverbial of time.

**d)** An adverbial of manner.

Which connective shows time in each of the sentences below?

**5** Finally the children were asleep.

**6** Meanwhile, all we could do was wait.

**7** Write down an adverbial of possibility to complete the sentence below.

I will _____ achieve full marks in our reading test tomorrow.

**8** Choose one word to add cohesion, which shows a paragraph is nearly finished.

**9** Order these modal verbs from less certain to more certain.

**will        might        must**

Choose a modal verb to make each sentence correct.

**10** We _____ have saved some money.

**11** They _____ pay before the session starts.

**12** I _____ have helped you.

**13** Where would the connective to 'summarise' go in a piece of report writing?

    **a)** At the beginning.

    **b)** In the middle.

    **c)** In the first paragraph.

    **d)** In the final paragraph.

Identify the adverbials of place in the sentences below.

**14** We are running towards the sea.

**15** John moved away from the snake very slowly.

Write a sentence for each of the modal verbs below.

**16** should

**17** shall

**18** could

**19** Identify the connective in the sentence below.

    I laughed out loud because the story was funny.

**20** Write down two ways you can add cohesion to your writing.

# Brackets and dashes

**Brackets**, **dashes** and **commas** can be used to insert a **parenthesis** into a sentence. A parenthesis is usually a word, phrase or clause that gives additional information.

We often put a parenthesis in **brackets** (brackets are also called **parentheses**).

**Example:**

The dog was last seen **(by an eye witness)** at the park.

If the brackets come at the end of the sentence, the full stop, exclamation mark or question mark normally goes **outside** the brackets.

**Example:**

The dog was last seen at the park **(by an eye witness)**.

We might decide to use **dashes** instead of brackets if the extra information needs **more emphasis**.

**Example:**

The dog was last seen – **by an eye witness** – at the park.

At the end of a sentence, only one dash is needed.

**Example:**

The dog was last seen at the park – **by an eye witness**.

Commas can be used instead of brackets and dashes. They give less of a clue as to how important the extra information is.

**Example:**

The dog was last seen, **by an eye witness,** at the park.

**1** Which two sentences below have **brackets** in the correct places?

**a)** London the capital city of England (is very popular).

**b)** (The climate) is getting warmer according to conservationists.

**c)** The music concert (in the local theatre) starts at five o'clock.

**d)** Reading books especially non-fiction (helps you to learn).

**e)** The programme (about whales) was very interesting.

## Test yourself

**2** Copy these sentences and add **brackets**.

**a)** Washington in America is where the President lives.

**b)** Ice skating although it is a bit dangerous is lots of fun.

**c)** Galleons Tudor ships were very big and slow.

**d)** Erin is a great singer or so she thinks!

**e)** February often rainy is the coldest month of the year.

## Challenge yourself

**3** Rewrite **three** of the sentences in question 2 using **dashes** instead of brackets.

**4** Copy the sentences below and add **commas**.

**a)** My birthday on August 29th makes me the youngest girl in my class.

**b)** The sun normally hiding was shining yesterday.

# Commas I

A **comma** is used to separate items in a list.

> **Example:**
>
> There will be sandwiches, fruit, biscuits, crisps and cakes.

Commas are also used to separate words in a sentence. They can replace brackets and separate added information.

> **Example:**
>
> My school, which is close to my house, has a long driveway.

A comma can also go between two clauses to make them easier to read.

> **Example:**
>
> She arrived at the train station, but the train had already gone.

## Warm up

1. Copy out these sentences, adding commas to the lists in them.

   a) I like English geography science music and art.

   b) Newcastle Liverpool Hartlepool and Leeds are all cities in the north of England.

   c) The Nile Amazon Mississippi Congo and Amur are some of the world's longest rivers.

   d) For lunch, we ate sandwiches crisps some cucumber and tomato and a biscuit.

   e) My friends are called Amos Seb Summer and Raj.

   f) The cinema is open on a Friday Saturday Sunday and Wednesday.

**2** Copy these sentences, placing commas in suitable places in them.

**a)** The children who were all aged 10 played at the park.

**b)** The boy stopped talking had a drink then started again!

**c)** When we arrived at the airport we found our flight had been cancelled.

**d)** I like skipping but my brother likes football.

**e)** My friends are all going ice skating but I have to go to the dentist.

**f)** Although I am good at spelling I still need to use a dictionary sometimes.

**g)** Our school which is one hundred years old this year had a special party.

## Challenge yourself

**3** Copy out and complete the sentences below by adding extra information. Remember to put commas in the correct places.

**a)** Our garden _____ faces south.

**b)** The bus station _____ was very busy.

**c)** My cousins _____ are coming to stay for a few days.

**d)** The doctor _____ arrived at the hospital.

**e)** My birthday present _____ is in my bedroom.

**f)** My mum _____ was going to the gym.

# Commas 2

Some sentences change their meaning depending on where the commas are placed, so commas need to be used carefully in order to make the meaning clear.

**Example:**

The people waiting who had tickets were let in.

Here, not everyone waiting had a ticket and was let in.

The people waiting, who had tickets, were let in.

Here, everybody waiting had a ticket and was let in.

**Warm up**

**1** **a)** Write down how many people climbed the tree in the sentences below.

   **i)** After they left Dad, James and Alicia climbed a tree.

   **ii)** After they left, Dad, James and Alicia climbed a tree.

   **b)** Write down how many people went for a walk in the sentences below.

   **i)** While they walked, Sam, Amy and Toby played with a yo-yo.

   **ii)** While they walked Sam, Amy and Toby played with a yo-yo.

   **c)** Write down how many people washed the car in the sentences below.

   **i)** After they left, Mum, Dad and their three friends washed the car.

   **ii)** After they left Mum and Dad, their three friends washed the car.

**2** Draw pictures to show you understand how the comma can change the meaning in the pairs of sentences below.

**a)** Mrs Ellis liked eating lots of foods: chocolate cake, fruit cake and strawberries were her favourite.

**b)** Mrs Ellis liked eating lots of foods: chocolate, cake, fruit cake and strawberries were her favourite.

**c)** "Let's eat Grandma!"

**d)** "Let's eat, Grandma!"

**Challenge yourself**

**3** Help police
Help, police!

**a)** Which of the above phrases gives the meaning the police want to be helped?

**b)** Which of the above phrases gives the meaning someone is in trouble and needs help from the police?

**4** Write down two of your own sentences to show how changing the position of commas can change the meaning of the sentence.

# Paragraphs

A **paragraph** is used to help organise information in a text. It usually contains one main topic and one or more sentences about this topic.

Paragraphs usually start with an **opening sentence**, which tells readers what the paragraph will be about. This opening sentence will then be explained and ideas will be developed as the writing continues.

> **Example:**
>
> Many people believe that the weather in Great Britain is often unpredictable. During the winter months it can be very cold and windy. There can also be a lot of rainfall, which occasionally may lead to localised flooding.

In **fiction**, a new paragraph is usually started when the writing changes to a new time, action, event, place or person.

In **non-fiction**, a new paragraph is started when a new point, topic, theme or fact is introduced.

## Warm up

**1** Look at the opening sentences from a range of paragraphs.

Decide if each paragraph will be fiction or non-fiction.

a) Many people believe that the weather in Great Britain is often unpredictable.

b) Later that day, a small parcel arrived through the post.

c) At long last, the boat reached the shore.

d) On the other hand, playtime is an important part of the school day.

e) The play area, located at the back of the park, should be supervised at all times.

f) Just then, the door swung open and looking rather worried, there stood Alya.

g) Henry VIII died in 1547.

h) There is a vast variety of wildlife in the rainforest.

2 Look at the opening sentences and complete the paragraphs using any facts or ideas that fit with the topic. The paragraphs must be clear and organised.

**a)** Many animals' habitats are disappearing.

**b)** A shadow mysteriously appeared from the corner of the room. The two boys stopped, terrified.

**c)** Some people prefer reading a book to watching films.

**d)** Several weeks later, the twins returned from their travels.

**Challenge yourself**

3 Write a **fact sheet** about a place of your choice. You could choose your hometown, a village or city, a holiday destination or a country.

Use **paragraphs** to organise your ideas. Include some of the following:

| |
|---|
| **Location** |
| **What is there to do?** |
| **Climate / weather** |
| **Any interesting facts** |
| **Who lives here?** |
| **Your opinion of the place** |

# Direct speech

**Direct speech** is what a speaker actually says, and is written with **inverted commas** round it. (These are also called **quotation marks** or **speech marks**.)

> **Examples:**
>
> "All dogs need exercising," Mum informed me.
>
> I replied grumpily, "I know!"
>
> "In that case," said Mum, "here's the lead!"

If a sentence begins with direct speech (like in the **first** and **third** sentences above), we add a comma, exclamation mark or question mark just **before** the closing inverted comma, and then usually let the reader know who said it.

If the sentence begins by telling us who is speaking (like in the **second** sentence above), a comma should appear **before** the speech begins. When the direct speech finishes, it should normally end with a full stop, question mark or exclamation mark just **before** the closing inverted comma.

Notice that a new line starts when a new person begins speaking, and all direct speech starts with a **capital letter**, except where a sentence of direct speech is **broken** by information about who is talking (like in the **third** sentence).

## Warm up

1) Which two sentences are punctuated correctly? Write them down.

   **a)** "Where's your homework?" the teacher asked.

   **b)** "If you finish," he said, "you'll make me very proud."

   **c)** "Oh, no!" The balloon has burst I cried.

   **d)** Amy said "Let's have a drink"

**2** Write out these sentences, and then add inverted commas and the correct punctuation.

**a)** Abbey said Don't worry

**b)** Nothing is wrong replied Dad

**c)** Maybe one day said Josh we'll play football for England

**d)** Help shouted the lost little girl Help

**Challenge yourself**

**3** Rewrite the sentences below using direct speech. Remember to punctuate them correctly.

**Example:** Mohammed asked Zack if he would like to play tennis after school.

Mohammed asked Zack, "Would you like to play tennis after school?"

**a)** Holly said that she couldn't wait to go on holiday next year.

**b)** Alfie told his teacher that he didn't understand the work.

**c)** The reporter announced that the restaurant had been shut down because of hygiene issues.

# Progress test 3

Write out the sentences below, adding two commas to make each correct.

**1** Football golf tennis and cricket are my favourite sports.

**2** A balanced diet which includes fruit and vegetables helps us to keep healthy.

**3** Which sentence uses inverted commas correctly?

a) The politician announced, "We will open new schools."

b) "The politician announced, "We will open new schools.

c) "The politician announced, We will open new schools."

d) The politician announced, "We will open new schools".

Where would you insert two sets of brackets in the sentences below, so that they are punctuated correctly?

**4** Sarah aged 11 produced some excellent artwork in the style of Monet a famous artist.

**5** Mario from Wolverhampton was last seen walking his dog in the park near the community centre.

Put the detective's words into direct speech, using inverted commas.

**6** The detective said there was a burglary this afternoon between the hours of 14.00 and 18.00, and he is looking for witnesses.

**7** The detective advised the chief inspector to arrest the man immediately.

**8** – **9** Write two sentences that use brackets for parenthesis.

Write out the lists below, adding commas in the correct places.

10  November December January and February are all winter months.

11  Cats rabbits dogs fish gerbils and hamsters are all pets.

12  I have visited lots of places including France Germany Spain and Italy.

13  Write out the sentence below, changing its meaning by adding correct punctuation and capitalisation.

  Stop ducks crossing road.

Write out the sentences below, adding dashes to make the sentences correct.

14  Computer games online can become quite addictive parents are warned.

15  The temperature according to the Met office is going to be higher than yesterday.

16  Copy out the sentence below, and add the missing punctuation.

  All children must write a letter as mentioned in assembly last week to invite their parents into school.

Add brackets to make the sentences below correct.

17  The school trip taking place in July will be a four-night residential.

18  My car a silver Vauxhall is at the garage.

19  Reporters local and national are at the scene.

20  Copy out the sentence and fill in the missing word.

  Paragraphs are used to _____ ideas and information.

Score ⬤/20   43

Published by Keen Kite Books
An imprint of HarperCollins*Publishers* Ltd
The News Building, 1 London Bridge Street,
London SE1 9GF

ISBN 9780008161408

Text and design © 2015 Keen Kite Books, an
imprint of HarperCollins*Publishers* Ltd

Author: Laura Griffiths